MENTAL TOUGHNESS TIPS AND TRICKS

How To Build Mental Toughness And Focus To Achieve Your Goals with Self-Control, Relentless, Resilience, Self-Awareness, Willpower, Wisdom, Self-Confidence And Emotional Intelligence

By Roman Power

Table of Contents

Introduction

A philosophy that was created many years ago, Stoicism is still incredibly helpful, even in the modern era. The stoic philosophy was derived to control emotions. A stoic person does not complain and can face hardships easily. Undoubtedly, stoicism can also be helpful in the endurance of pain. Becoming a stoic can be difficult, but through this technique, you can master your thoughts. This philosophy can make you stronger, and emotional turmoil will not affect you if you can learn how to behave as a stoic does.

Many great people, one of whom was the Roman king Marcus Aurelius, have practiced it. The emperor was a paradoxical example of stoicism. Another famous historical person was Epictetus, and beyond him there are many more examples.

You can master your thoughts and improve your energy. Doesn't it seem fantastically empowering to get to know yourself better, control your thoughts in a way that benefits you, and find harmony in life? Stoicism embraces acceptance, and whether the outcome of any situation is good or bad it keeps you calm. It teaches you to accept reality.

According to science, the human mind is full of memories. However, where does this memory come from? I'd say experience rather than thoughts. There can be certain experiences that create specific thoughts. For instance, a trauma during childhood may never be forgotten. This trauma can give your thoughts an everlasting impression. Thoughts are the fundamentals of human nature. You are what you think. Perception makes a huge difference.

Thoughts, feelings, emotions, and hormones give birth to some sort of energy within the body. It could be positive energy or negative energy. Stoicism shuts down negative thoughts and negative behaviors. It promotes a positive attitude towards life. It lets you see reality for what it really is and helps you with acceptance, too. Ultimately, stoicism changes one's mindset.

Chapter 1:
Acting Like A Stoic

One of the main tenets that guide the Stoic mind is a discipline that goes beyond the definitions that are usually attached to it. We define discipline in ways that seem medieval and harsh. We see discipline as something that is lacking and deserves punishment. We see discipline as the harder voice to the playful self.

Our faulty idea of discipline and the eventual inability to invoke it puts us in the path of many consequences that distract and derail us, and so those who do master discipline manage to walk a hamstrung/straight jacket life.

But that is not the discipline we need, nor the discipline that Stoics practice. Stoic discipline is easy to institute because it is based on truth and reality. It is based on the understanding of our bodies and the habits of our minds.

We often get confused with the true nature of discipline. It has no wonder that that happens when that term has been repeatedly pounded into us in the classroom and living room.

When we do not do what we must, we are accused of lacking discipline. When we do something we should not, we are chided for not being disciplined. There are so many ways to use the word and none of them seem to be pleasant. It leaves us with this foul taste in our mouth, like penicillin without the protection of the dissolvable capsule.

But just like penicillin, it has its benefits—while the downside is merely superficial.

Let us erase all that and rekindle our association with this term.

Habits

We live our life in a time when the ghost of our evolutionary past makes some things difficult for us to do.

Think of a habit. When you have a habit, it is a really a string of three things that happen. There is a cue, a response, and a reward. When you drive to work and you come to a stoplight, that instantly triggers the response of turning in the direction you need to proceed. Making the correct turn makes you feel that all is well in the world. If you make the wrong turn, you feel awful—negative reinforcement.

Let us look at something more. Let us say you smoke every day after a meal. As soon as you are done with your meal, the habit to light up is triggered, and that gives you, in addition to the nicotine, pleasure. You see the pattern—trigger, followed by response.

Everything forms some form of habit—even behavior, people (seeing someone, hearing their voice, and so on), things, experiences.

Withdrawal is a negative habit. If you are used to one thing, even though you do not get the pleasure of seeing it or experiencing it, you will feel it in the event that it is absent. It is a category of habit that uses negative reinforcement.

These forces that act on you can have a debilitating effect and they can be a distraction. Smoking as a hobby is pleasant to enjoy; smoking to relieve a habit is a distraction. Gambling for the fun of it is invigorating, but gambling to satisfy a habit is a vice. Sex as part of a marriage can be necessitated by the desire to have offspring. Sex can also be for the enjoyment of pleasure. But sex that is demanded to satisfy a craving repeatedly is unhealthy.

We think of all these things in terms of balance. The need for food, in balance, is healthy. The greed for food, in abundance, is fatal.

Stoics are not prone to scratching an itch. They do things for the efficacy or for the enjoyment, but they never allow it to control them. Any form of control over one's actions leads to unintended and negative consequences that in itself can be a distraction to things in the future. So, the execution of the act because of the need to satisfy this kind of habit erodes the strength of the mind and causes distractions in the present, and distraction in the future when the time comes to pay the piper.

Moderation in all you do is essential and to get the moderation going, you need a kind of discipline.

Let me illustrate.

I was raised as far back as I can remember to wake up at 5:30 a.m. There was no such thing as days off or on. It was not predicated on the day of the week or the season of the year. In our household that is just the way it was. My father would be up at 4:30; my mother, soon after that, and by the time I was up, the house would be bustling with activity, the smell of coffee, the aroma of my father's tobacco, and the cacophony of sounds emanating from pots, pans, dishes, mugs, and cutlery.

All through college, while I was away from home, no matter how late I hit the sack, I would be up at 5:30. The question then is this: Was that a habit or was that the result of discipline?

It is a habit and not a discipline. But for many people waking up at 6:30 requires the discipline of a monk. It is not part of them to wake up at a certain time of day. One of my roommates in college (briefly) could not wake up till 10 minutes before his first class—which he went out of his way to schedule no earlier than 10 a.m. Do not get me wrong, he did well in life—this is not a story of waking up early and doing well because of it. He went on to build a successful startup after college and since then he has become a serial entrepreneur with four IPOs under his belt. He still wakes up at 10 a.m.

The point is about habits and discipline. Habits come naturally—and you should cherish habits if you have got the good ones. But discipline is the force that you use to alter the trajectory of those habits. Look at it this way. Think of the space shuttle that is on a trajectory. Its inertia is carrying it on a given trajectory—what is required to alter that trajectory or to bring it to a stop? Well, that is what those thrusters are for in the front of its nose. A little blast here, a little blast there, and you get minor course corrections that alter its trajectory. That is discipline.

Changing Trajectory

Discipline is the force that moves the inertia you have gained. So if you have taken on a habit of smoking—that sway the habit has on you is a trajectory that will move your life, and if you do nothing else, that trajectory will chart a course across your life. But to alter that habit requires that you apply minor course corrections to get you out of that trajectory.

With that overview in mind, let us look at the discipline of a Stoic and see the areas that it is applied, how it is applied, and to what end.

A Stoic's discipline is unforced. It is natural and this is unfamiliar to the rest of those of us who aspire to live the Stoic way. No Stoic feels discipline as something that is forced and painful, requiring effort, sacrifice, and suffering. It's like a child forced to do homework while his favorite cartoon plays for the one and only time on TV. And just like the kid who is forced to do something because of misplaced priorities, we feel the pain when required to do the right thing.

It is a matter of perspectives, isn't it? It's like the game show where the host knows what's behind the door, but the contestant doesn't, and he is filled with worry and chaos as he tries to choose the right door. But for the host, the choice is obvious.

A parent and child have the same interactive relationship, the older knowing what is best, the younger knowing what is fun. The Stoic and the non-Stoic have the same relationship. The Stoic is loyal to the best course of action; the rest struggle with what feels good.

But there really isn't a choice, is there? The course of action is typically known and appreciated, but it is the cacophony of distractions that make the action untenable. We mistake this as wisdom in many cases when all it really is, is misplaced priorities and the lack of discipline to correct the course deviation.

So, the question remains. What is a Stoic's discipline? As you may have started to uncover, the Stoic's discipline is about loyalty to doing the right thing. So what? Why is the right thing so important? Because the right thing is paid for or rewarded in the future. You can think of it as an annuity. You deposit something now and it pays off slowly over time. Discipline is about making the choice so that you maximize that slow payout in the future. You do what is necessary now so that all that unfolds over the course of time accrues as benefit. Doing the wrong thing now, no matter how pleasurable, yields a series of unfortunate catastrophes that snowball over time. Sometimes it even passes from one's own life and into the life of one's children.

Before we go any further, perhaps now is good a time as any to make one thing clear about the Stoic's worldview. There is no right and wrong when it comes to the Stoic's perspective—at least not in the sense that the rest see it.

No Right or Wrong

The Stoic's core tenet is that there is no good or bad, no right or wrong. But even without this binary set of choices, they are able to come out ahead in most scenarios. How is that even possible? Because it turns out that this universe is not built on right and wrong but on chaos and peace. There is a delicate balance of chaos and peace that pervades the fabric of everything that makes up this universe—everything that we can detect, and everything that we can't. This universe is a balance of chaos and silence. But do not make the mistake of thinking that one is energy and the other, a void. Both are forms of energy, and when in balance, they cancel each other out. But that balance is elusive and constantly oscillates from one state to the other.

It is like a pendulum moving from a point of dynamic imbalance to momentary equilibrium and then back again. This, in the view of a Stoic, is the metronome of the universe. Everything else big, small, and immeasurable, follows this pace. That includes all things tangible and all things intangible. From the balance of night and day, to the beat of the heart, to the vibrations of the atom, to the waxing and waning from inspiration to depression.

This allows the Stoic to see things differently, and it's not just a perspective. The way they see it encompasses most of all the perspectives, and they see it in an almost omnipotent way—I say "almost" because it would be impossible to see it all absolutely—there are perspectives that we are unable to perceive and experience without the necessary senses.

When you speak to a Stoic, and many have said this about men, including Marcus Aurelius, you may feel like the Stoic is able to see right through you and is not far from the truth. When you distill all things down to this chaos and peace framework, you start to understand the landscape of motivations each person has and the actions that flow from those motivations. When you are in that state, it is not hard to see why people do the things they do. It's like a parent who can see through the shenanigans of the child even before they think of doing something.

When you see discipline through this framework then it no longer looks like the baggage of effort that we think needs to be carried in order to get something done. Discipline then just becomes what it is—the conviction to do the right thing.

Stoics are composed and stoic—as the name implies, not because they are forcing themselves to be uncaring, but because they see a higher game at play, and the minor variances of feelings and emotions are just not perceptible to their senses, nor are they prioritized in their consciousness.

It is not just the way one looks at things, but the way one fosters his or her state of being. Think about the state of a child who wants to stay up past his bedtime and does not get his parents' approval. The parents know that the short-term benefit of going to bed late in no way outweighs the long-term benefit of rest and forming good habits for a young child. And so, the tears of the child don't even come close to figuring into the responsible parent's decision. It is similar to how a Stoic sees most things.

Being in State

But what has all this got to do with discipline? The state you are in has everything to do with discipline. If you are not in the state to do something then you need a huge amount of effort to do it, and the outcome is not nearly as probable as it would be if you are in the right state. A Stoic's state is one that matches the task that he is about to undertake—no matter how devastating his surroundings or his circumstances.

When you are in this state, you do not need to force yourself to do the things that need to be done. You do not need the discipline to bend your hesitance into will. You do not need to force the tasks necessary to accomplish the final goal. As such, when you are in this state, the future unfolds almost effortlessly.

Just like everything else, our decision-making process is also a habit. Each individual takes a specific path in coming to a decision and then coming to an action plan. There are two kinds of decisions, the first being the ones we plan on doing, and the second ones being the ones we actually execute. In many cases they are one and the same, but in a number of people what is planned is never what is executed. For a Stoic, what is executed is what was planned.

Think of the decision-making process as a path; it is just like the path you take when you drive to the store or the office. It is predictable and it is habitual. A person doesn't make bad decisions because he wants to face difficulty; a person makes bad decisions because he doesn't know any other path to take from where he stands to the point of the action.

While we look at discipline as the effort to push an action, a Stoic's discipline is about moving from one state to the next, depending on the task and goal at hand.

How does one make that happen?

If you are looking to understand Stoicism, there are a few books you can turn to, the most important being Meditations, by Emperor Marcus Aurelius. Even that book was not something that Emperor Marcus chose to publish. It wasn't until much later that historians compiled his notes and placed them in book form. There are very few books that were written on this topic, fewer still that were translated well, and even fewer that have lasted till today.

What we do have are those who are innately Stoic who guide us with the principles of Stoicism. Then there are those of us who spend years reflecting, studying, testing and pushing the boundaries of what is considered life.

I encourage you to read as many interpretations as you can to get a better grasp of the many facets that encompass the Stoic's life.

Let's get back to the discipline of a Stoic.

To bring the Stoic's discipline into your life the first thing you need to do is embrace the ideals of a Stoic.

Peace and truth are not what you used to think they were.

A Stoic is the embodiment of peace. Peace is not just the reward one gets for behaving and thinking in a certain way; peace is the state that reflects calm and understanding. Let's be clear: peace is also not about bending backwards and letting others trample over you. Peace is about knowing the secrets of nature and how things unfold.

Let's take, for instance, the concept of death. We all know that it exists, yet we are never prepared for it when it comes. Or are we?

Simple. Discipline, to most of us, is hard because we see it as the force required to change the trajectory of our decision-making process. The Stoic sees it as part and parcel of the outcome.

Chapter 2:
Focus on What You Can Control Only

Oftentimes, fear, anxiety, stress, depression and frustration are rooted in our desire to control everything around us. We want everything to be perfect and just the way we want. This pursuit makes us worry about everything and often become fixated on our past or future. We keep thinking on how things could have been or how things can be, but completely fail to pause and think of how things can be in this very moment.

Our need to control our future and to worry relentlessly about our past makes us completely disregard our present. We forget that it is our present we are living in and it is the moments that we are letting slip by that we should focus on. Not only that, but when we do try to focus on our present and make things work as we want, we try to control everything around us. The pursuit of perfectionism turns us into control freaks when we try to do everything perfectly, but often our efforts end in vain. We fail to understand that there are only certain things in our control; things pertinent to us and we cannot at any cost control every external factor.

When we see things not going, as we want, we become frustrated and sad, which often triggers our different fears and gives birth to a negative mindset. This clouds our judgment and the ability to perceive things rationally and keeps us from becoming completely virtuous. In addition, oftentimes, it is our fears and the desire to control everything that makes us resort to unjust means of doing things and dealing unfairly with others. To overcome these issues to allow happiness in your life for good, learn to focus only on what you can control.

There are only certain things that are up to us and within our control; everything else lies outside our domain of power. Our judgments, actions and thoughts are the only things up to us. These are our own voluntary choices and everything else that does not fall in these categories is beyond our control.

You can only work on controlling your thoughts which then influence your judgments and beliefs, which then shape your decisions, actions and behavior. For instance, if you think you can be happy with only the essentials in life and do not need to rely on any material possession, you will soon nurture this belief. This very belief will change the way you perceive material gains and soon you will stop working hard to acquire them but will instead focus on improving your actions and finding pleasure in the moment to be happy.

As you stop worrying about the things you cannot control and focus your energy, time and effort on improving everything within your reach and power, you let go of unnecessary stress, frustrations, anger, negativity and fears in life. When you know there is no point fretting over why your best friend doesn't spend time with you, because you cannot control him, you look for other ways to spend your time. As you let go of your dependency on your friend, you free yourself of undue stress and feel calm.

Moreover, the realization that you can control your own thoughts, actions and judgments to live better is quite a huge confidence booster. You do all in you might to achieve what you want and since you know you have given a goal your very best, you feel happy about it.

Understand that your life is like that of an archer: you have things like the type of bow and arrow to use, the direction to set the arrow in and when to strike it in your control.

Be Aware of Your Genuine Needs

With time as you become more aware of your thoughts; focus on finding out your genuine needs. This is important so that you know what you wish to strive for and what really matters to you.

Oftentimes, we stress ourselves for things we do not really yearn for and this keeps us from becoming truly virtuous. We think we want a big house and a luxury car and do everything within and beyond our control to achieve it only to end up feeling stressed after achieving those material gains.

Awareness of your genuine needs makes you more mindful of yourself, which helps you shift your focus from the meaningless stuff happening around you and strive for things you believe in. This helps you become a rational and virtuous being.

Treat the Past as a Bygone

What has happened, has happened and you need to let go of that. You cannot travel back in time and when that is not possible, it is futile to worry about things that have happened.

Let go of all your regrets and open wounds pertinent to your past so you can become more attentive towards your present. Recall those memories and imagine them burning into ashes.

Play this visualization into your head. It might take some time, but you will get there and feel better. Practice this daily to remind yourself of how every moment that passes away will not return and that you should concentrate on your present only.

Everyone is Entitled to Live as They Want

At times in life, we experience the desire to control all those related to us in one way or another especially those we love. While often, such feelings are rooted in our best intentions for others, but what we ignore is the fact that everyone is born free and is entitled to hold their own opinions.

Learn to Settle for Good Enough

Perfectionism is a trap, one that only cripples your confidence and good judgment. When you work on a task, opt for good enough instead of making things perfect because nothing is and can be perfect.

If you are working on a project and you miss out on a few details or even a big point, don't punish yourself for it. It is okay to make mistakes and not do things completely right.

Letting Go of Control in Our Lives

How many times in your life do you deal with anger or anxiety? Even if it is not something that has been diagnosed as a problem in your life, it is still something that a lot of people deal with on a daily basis. They are anxious when things go against their plan, they get anxious when they get in a situation, they are not able to control, and when this anxiety starts to come around, they feel anger at the same time.

Accept Things the Way They Are

Learn to not control everything around you. No matter how much you try, you are not the one in control of everything. This is hard for some people to accept, but the sooner you do, the sooner you will be able to enjoy true happiness. The only thing that you can be in control of is your own actions and thoughts, and the rest you just have to let go of.

Rather than letting our emotions get in the way and make us unhappy and letting those emotions get in the way of our happiness, it is time to learn how to just let go. It will do so much good for everyone, but especially for you. It may be hard, but the principles of Stoicism will help this become a reality in no time.

Ego and Stoicism

We as a whole have contemplation, emotions, driving forces and recollections that can be hard to manage. In other words, it is wearying. At times, people manage such emotions by using what is known as defense systems. These resistance components are oblivious rational responses or effects that shield people from emotions of tension or anxiety, insecurities to one-self, and things that they would prefer not to consider or manage. They feel uncomfortable and weak.

The personality of someone is the character of their mind and it is one's own development, a bogus, phony or fake personality. We are something other than the reasoning we do with our brains. If we take into consideration; of every one of the convictions of what we are – convictions about our character, gifts, and capacities – we have the structure of our sense of self. These gifts, capacities, and parts of our character will be properties of our aptitudes; however, the psychological development of our "self" is pretentious, and keeping in mind that this depiction may cause the inner self, our inner egoistical to appear to be a static thing, it is not, Or perhaps, it is a functioning and self-motivated piece of our characters, expecting a huge job in making enthusiastic show in our lives or some may show-off. At the point when we have contemplations about our self that we concur with we develop a mental self-image or egoistical figure.

At the point when we have such considerations and concur with even the scarcest conviction that these thoughts characterize us, at that point, we are assembling, or fortifying, an inner self. We initially have these considerations when we are kids, maybe when we were prodded on the play area, or when denounced or adulated by an educator or parent.

In all societies, building up a mental self-portrait is a typical piece of socialization. Issues emerge, nonetheless, when that mental self-view is negative, wrong, or even excessively positive. Taking into account that we build up our idea of "self" as youngsters, it is inescapable that our mental self-view doesn't guide to reality as grown-ups.

The sense of self keeps us from following up on our essential desires yet additionally attempts to accomplish an offset with our good and hopeful measures.

While the sense of a person works in both, preconscious and conscious, its solid connections to the id (The brain where natural intuitive driving forces and essential procedures are manifest) implies that it additionally works in the oblivious.

In some cases, it takes a gander at the first wellspring of these plans to improve the point of view on the problem. Scientists expounded broadly on the sense of self just as its relationship to different parts of the character.

- Unmasking ego

For what reason is the sense of right and wrong so difficult to clarify or describe? The inner self is hard to characterize because the personality isn't one explicit thing. It is comprised of various convictions that an individual secures over their life. Those convictions can be different and even opposing. To further confound it, every individual's conscience is unique. If somebody were to unmistakably distinguish and portray every one of the pieces of their sense of self and what it drives them to do, you probably won't get a decent depiction of what yours resembled. The test of getting mindful of what your sense of self resembles turns out to be increasingly troublesome because our way of life doesn't remunerate us for coordinating our consideration internal and seeing such things.

The conscience is hard to see since it takes cover behind sentiments that show up apparent – our connection to depictions of our character – and because we have not worked on studying. You can get a look by seeing certain considerations, like those recorded previously. The simpler method to recognize the personality is by the trail of emotional acknowledgments it decamps anger at a friend or family member, a should be correct, an inclination of instability in specific circumstances, sentiments of envy that are unexplained, the need to intrigue somebody, etc. These feelings can be ascribed to the swindles that include the sense of self. To start with, it is simpler to see the side effects of coming about feelings and show, as opposed to the self-image that caused it.

- How stoicism relates ego?

The Stoics were not unacquainted with dreadful people. They saw leaders. They saw tricks. They saw poisonous egomaniacs and unquenchable desires. What is more, what was their response to the greater part of these people? Imagine what they could acquire by mending the motion of their emotions.

Besides a general attentiveness and a craving not to be defiled by them, for the most part, the Stoics felt sorry for these sorts. Absolutely, this is the means by which Marcus Aurelius expounded on somebody like Alexander the Great. He nearly appeared to be pitiful for him. Like, seriously dude, how could you think this was going to end? Did you think vanquishing the world was going to satisfy you? Did you really believe that popularity and greatness would fill that gap in your spirit?

It is a wise and philosophical attitude towards those ignorant; Egomaniacs do not make it easy for us to pity them rather they make fun of them and enjoy. It does not even affect inquisitors or crooks; they feel harmless about this. Particularly when their success comes at the cost of our blood and sweat, nonetheless the truth is, they can't help themselves at this point. It is not even any fun to be like them. There is no pressure, but they do not feel anything about them. It is not a game.

Given the manner in which that the irrelevant notice of anxiety makes most fearful or depleted, "stoicism facts" externally appears as though the definite inverse thing anyone would need to get some answers concerning, also desperately require for the duration of regular daily existence. Nevertheless, truth be told, in Stoicism, we have a mechanical assembly to help us as we continued looking for self-predominance, ingenuity, and savvy: something one uses to continue with an inconceivable life, rather than some dark field of insightful solicitation. In it, we find without a doubt the most imperative adroitness all through the whole presence of the world. Sometimes, people question where does this ego come from? Where exactly?

We feel it from everything and everybody, including our own nature.

At the point when we are obstructing personality, we are haughty, childish, and silly. We are mean, we are shallow, we are shaky, and we are delicate. To put it plainly, we are everything a Stoic should be.

"It is difficult to discover what we think we definitely know," Epictetus said. That is the reason we stay away from a sense of self. Marcus discussed dodging the stain of "imperialization"- - the conscience that would originate from being head and having power. He discussed the silliness of attempting to make yourself associated with a thousand years or of reasoning you'll live until the end of time. Both these insightful

31

and effective men were doing a steady fight against their inner selves, as all Stoics have attempted to do as the centuries progressed.

We cannot work with other individuals in the event that we have set up dividers. We cannot improve the world on the off chance that we don't get it or ourselves. We cannot make or get criticism on the off chance that we are unequipped for or uninterested in got notification from outside sources. We can't perceive possibilities—or make them—if as objected to seeing what is before us, we live inside our dreams. Without a precise bookkeeping of our capacities contrasted with others, what we have isn't certainty yet hallucination. How are we expected to reach, propel, or lead other individuals in the event that we can't identify with their needs—since we've put some distance between our own?

The Greeks realized that ego; the sense of self by another name was a definitive adversary and an enemy of oneself. That nothing but must have to be controlled. That being timid and having self-awareness were genuine quality, the untruth facts of our lives. We have to recall the equivalent. That is the reason we need to make and understanding with this.

"We're selfish with property and cash, yet barely care about sitting around idly, the one thing about which we should all be the hardest penny pinchers." — Seneca

The Stoics comprehended that time is our most noteworthy resource that should be under our consideration. In contrast to any of our material belongings and possessions that we hold, when lost, time can never be recaptured. We should consequently endeavor to squander as meager of it as could reasonably be expected.

Tomorrow isn't guaranteed!

Then again, the people who openly give away their time to others will likewise find that they are no superior to anything the individuals who waste it. The greater part of us enables people and different duties to force on our time too effectively. We make responsibilities without giving a profound idea to what it involves. Schedules and timetables were intended to support us. We ought not to become captive to them.

Notwithstanding which end of the range we fall into; time is of the essence. We think we have a ton of time, yet we truly don't have another choice regarding this. A lot of what we do come from our basic should be loved and acknowledged by others. Dissatisfaction from our social gathering had genuine repercussions previously. It would have likely implied outcast and death in the wilderness. That is still consistent with some degree today. Be that as it may, what amount of time and exertion do we spend attempting to win the endorsement of others?

Chapter 3:
Stoicism in Pain Management

"He who is brave is free."

A nyone who tells you that pain is just a state of mind should be smacked in the head—or better still, sent to a labor ward to watch a woman give birth to a child. Pain is a reaction to physical, mental, or emotional hurt. And it is a perfectly natural process. However, with the implementation of Stoic principles, you can control the intensity of the pain you feel, as well as the extent of the damage it may cause. It is a very difficult concept to accept, but it is not as foreign as we think. We have heard stories of brilliant people who work with intelligence agencies and are trained to withstand the most gruesome forms of torture without breaking. People who work in the military, air force, or navy are rumored to undergo similar pain management training in the event of their capture. Now, we are not going all gung-ho on this like people who work with government security agencies, but there are some kinds of pain that do need to be managed.

There are two major types of pain that we experience: emotional pain and physical pain. In my opinion, all pain stems from these two types of pain, and if you can equip yourself to deal with it, you are in a better position to deal with all of the other stuff. But before we get into it, there is something you need to bear in mind. Pain is not your enemy.

Don't make it your mission to seek out ways to numb yourself. There is a reason your body and mind were built with pain receptors. They can help you recognize your limits. Without those pain receptors, you run the risk of hurting yourself beyond repair. Without pain, you lose the ability to function like a normal human being. In a world that glorifies superheroes, we may aspire for a life where we live beyond the reach of pain. But if you look closely, you will see that your favorite heroes hurt, too. They do not live beyond pain; they have simply learned to live above it. Embrace your pain, and when you do, you will reclaim the power it has over you.

Physical Pain

Don't let anyone tell you that the pain you are feeling is all in your head. We all experience pain at different levels. My six could be your two and your 10 could be someone else's five. This is not something to get into a competition over. It is just one of those realities that you are going to have to embrace. That said, there are several techniques that can be used to manage physical pain without relying on medication. These practices date back millennia. Women employed these techniques to help them cope with the pains of labor. Obviously, women have a lot of pain relief options for this now, but in the past, all they had was a cloth to chomp on and some mind games to get them through it. I am not even going to try and compare the pains of a woman in labor to anything, because I have been told that unless you are going through it, you are not going to understand it. Instead, I will use a more relatable kind of pain. And I found that in one of the greatest emperors that Rome had ever known: Marcus Aurelius.

Now, here was a man who suffered from chronic stomach ulcers, which prevented him from eating certain foods and eating at certain times. He was also known to experience chest pains and had issues sleeping. It is hard to accurately diagnose what Marcus was going through but suffice it to say that he was in an incredible amount of pain, which he lived with for most of his life. His resilience has been attributed to his Stoic training. In a few short steps, you can build your own mental resilience towards pain.

1. Don't judge the pain

We have a tendency to identify pain as bad, but when you do that, you develop a knee-jerk response to it that can distress you even more. So, step one is to step off the judgment box. As I pointed out earlier, pain is not your enemy. Neither is it your friend. Detach your judgment of the pain from the experience of it.

2. Change your perspective

Pain does not really harm you in the stoic sense, as it does not hurt your morals. What affects you, though, is how you react to it—and wallowing in pain is considered a negative reaction. So, if it is not truly harming you in the areas that matter, can it really hurt you? The answer is no—not unless you let it. In other words, pain requires your permission to truly cause harm.

3. Stay in the present

There are two things you need to consider when managing your pain. The first is your perceived ability to cope with it, and the second thing is your perception of the pain's severity. If you think the pain is too great and you cannot cope, chances are your anticipation of the pain will heighten the pain itself. Stop panicking and get your mind to relax. Stay focused on each moment, because each moment will get you through the next.

These Stoic techniques help build your mental resilience as well as your endurance level. You can pair them with physical pain-relief methods like focused breathing and meditation exercises. Other things you can do to complement your efforts include journaling your pain. We know of the physical travails of Marcus Aurelius because he wrote about his experiences. This gives you a better understanding of what you are dealing with.

The more understanding you have, the better equipped you are to cope with it. Medical experts also recommend maintaining a healthy lifestyle, which includes less alcohol, more exercise (which release endorphins, the body's natural painkiller), and a balanced diet.

Emotional Pain

If you thought measuring physical pain was difficult, the complicated nature of emotional pain will leave you very confused. Saying that we are all genetically wired in different ways is stating an obvious fact, but this plays into how we handle our emotions, as well. We react to emotional traumas differently, and sometimes, our reactions to these traumas can limit our ability to function as a human being. I have had days when getting out of bed seems to be the most tasking thing I can handle. People suffering from depression may reach a point in their emotional pain when living no longer seems like a viable option. People whose emotional pain was triggered by a physical trauma describe themselves as being stuck in the place of their trauma. For them, life seems to have stopped from the very day they experienced that traumatic event. They feel frozen in time, burdened by the pain and trapped in their nightmare. This is the extent of the damage that can be caused by emotional pain.

It is very possible to experience excruciating emotional pain with no physical evidence. You can mask your pain with a smile, and that is what makes it more dangerous than physical pain. On the flip side, there are emotional pains that can manifest physically. I have heard of medical cases where the patient's emotional distress presented as a heart attack. The doctors were able to address the emergency and patch the patient up, but there are no pills or surgeries that can help you deal with the pain that is inside your head. However, if we adopt the Stoic principle that urges us to change our perspective, we can see this as a huge advantage. For starters, the absence of pills to help you get rid of your pain means that you can step into that void and be your own pill.

Being in a state of emotional pain means you are no longer in harmony with your true nature, and we know how important it is in Stoicism to maintain that balance. The obvious solution would be to restore that balance and get you back in tune with nature. Kick start the process by doing the following:

1. Accept the reality of your experience

I am not talking about amor fati or loving fate here. I am referring to the fundamental Stoic principle that tells us our experiences are neither good nor bad. Rather, they fall into the category of one of those indifferent things that are not regarded as a vice or a virtue. It is a neutral external factor that can only harm you if you let it. Yes, what happened to you is tragic and painful, and you would love for that fact to be recognized but dwelling on it only amplifies its hold over you. This is the reality you need to awaken yourself to.

2. Recognize the limits

When we think limits, our first thought is ourselves and the boundaries that we must be conscious of. But the events around us also have their limits. They can trigger distress, cause significant pain, and temporarily create a disruption in your life—but that is as far as they can go.

However tragic it was, it cannot truly harm you. Ultimately, you have the power to shut it down.

3. Take Plato's view as your stand

Don't narrow down your entire life's journey to this single painful moment. You have an amazing life ahead of you, and it only takes a shift in focus from the present pain to the powerful possibilities that life has to offer for you to acknowledge this. Life can take you through several twists and turns, but there is no single moment that defines you. You are the one who defines the moment.

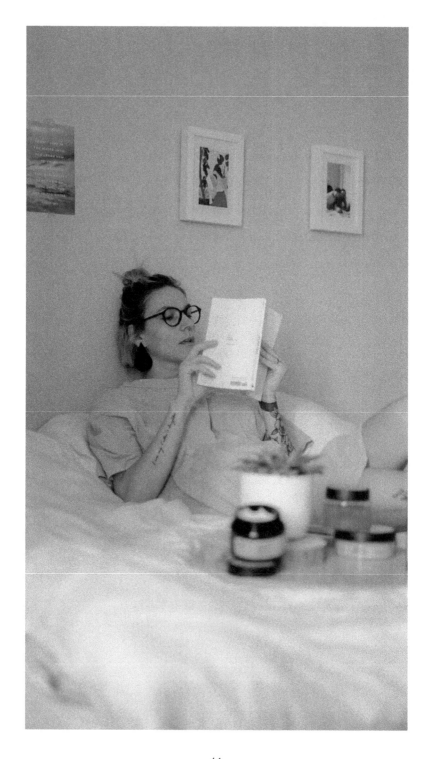

Chapter 4:
Stoicism and Happiness - The Stoic Triangle

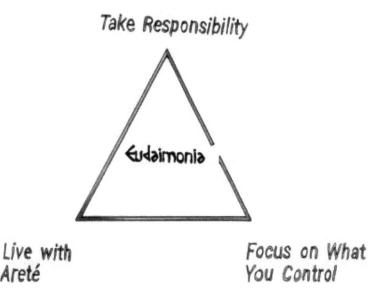

D o you realize that at the end of the day, we really only have control over one thing? We don't have control over the weather, over the actions of other people, or on our genetics, nor over our past. None of that! But we can control our minds. We can't control the external, but we can control our thoughts and with our thoughts, we can influence our emotions and control our actions. Even that alone can be extremely powerful. The key here with stoicism is to keep in mind that there is the only thing that we can control. Most people go through similar kind of things their entire lives and they go around thinking or not even thinking. They just kind of go around through their daily lives as if they have control over everything or rather worrying about everything external. They worry about the opinions of others, they worry about what the weather is going to be like, they worry about this or that, or they blame their genetics or their past or where they were born.

But the thing is, stoics realize that the only thing that we really can control is our minds. With that realization, the only thing that's really worth even focusing on or putting our time and energy into is optimizing our thoughts and having a high-quality mindset. That will lead to a life and a lifestyle that can breed peace of mind, happiness, and confidence.

We have to keep in mind that what we need to do on a daily routine is to realize that. We shouldn't focus on or worry about anything outside of our control. So, the next time something happens to you that's outside of your control, whether it's the weather, bad luck, or whatever it is, just keep in mind that the thing was bound to happen.

How you react to the situation really defines your character, and really will end up boiling down to more confidence for you. So, if you do get into a car crash, or if something bad happens to you, remember how you have to respond to the situation. If you stay cool, calm, and calculated in that situation and you don't really stress about it, you don't really worry, and you still focus on the other good things that are going to come to you throughout your day, then afterward you know it's going to actually be easier for you to continue to focus on your thoughts and on your mind.

Stoicism and Happiness

Through stoicism, you are going to learn the exact method to raise your default level of happiness. I'm not talking about happiness from external objects like money or fame or anything like that. I'm talking about increasing your level of joy, so you have this deep-rooted fulfillment that gives you pleasure at every moment of life, regardless of what your external circumstances are. Let us start with a quote from Seneca, who was a great philosopher back 2,000 years ago. According to him, true happiness is all about enjoying the present moment.

Someone who is not anxious about the future is also happier on the inside. Seneca said that someone who can be satisfied with what he already has is the real human. A human who has every contentment inside him. True happiness can be experienced by avoiding being anxious and without depending on the future. Seneca has told us so many things about being happy.

But don't get confused and think that Seneca is telling us that we shouldn't better ourselves or shouldn't aspire to gain material possessions in this world. This isn't the case, because Seneca himself was a very wealthy man. What he is telling us is actually an admonition against the lack of presence. People tend to forget about the present moment. We're always looking into the future and we're always looking into the past. We're always wishing for things, trying to get the next best thing and are never content with our lot. We suffer from the monkey mind, the distracted mind that lacks focus.

Of course, this is part of the human condition, and this is part of the social narrative. We are always thinking ahead, thinking of the family, our jobs, something we want to buy, or retirement. But the trap is that we miss out on living. We miss out on the present moment. Happiness is now. I really don't want you to get confused by this quote, thinking that Seneca is advising us not to want external things like money or happiness from external objects. If Seneca won the lottery, of course, he'd accept it. Seneca was a very wealthy man, so naturally he wouldn't advocate for less.

That's not the point. Instead, the point is to be content with what you have before you start looking for external things. To increase your happiness, Seneca is advising us to be completely present in the moment, stop thinking about the past, and stop thinking about the future.

Neither of those things is real, because in the future that moment in time will be the present moment. You can't change the past, for it's done, and you can't change the future because it hasn't happened yet. All you have is the present moment, so live now in this present moment. Get into the present moment and be aware of your surroundings.

Be aware that you're sitting down. Feel the scene, whether you are sitting on the bed or a couch or a chair. Sit and just be in the present moment. Take this time now to enjoy what you have. Stop thinking about the past, stop worrying about the future, and just be present right now. Whilst reading this book, appreciate that you have this time alone and that you have your computer or phone or wherever screen you're using. Just be completely present.

What happens over time is, our monkey mind gets completely distracted. It's only within our brain that we get an increase in happiness from external objects. Say, for example, you win the lottery and after some time your happiness increases a little bit. But after a week or a month or a year, your happiness goes back down to the default level. This is called the hedonic treadmill in science, and it states that whenever an external event happens to you, your happiness changes for a little bit. Whether it be a positive change or a negative change, after time you return to the default level of happiness.

This is just human nature, and this is what happens. This is why so many lottery winners enjoy the money for a certain length of time. After a while, their expectations increase, which brings the default level of happiness back down to where they were before they won the lottery. It's exactly the same thing if something negative happens. Say something is stolen from you. For a while you're annoyed at yourself, thinking why did I let this happen? But then, as time goes on, you return to your default level of happiness.

The advice that Seneca is giving you is to increase that level of happiness. To stop fluctuating between happiness and negative raises the bar completely. So, you can be completely content and completely joyful at all times. Let's reflect back. Think of when you were younger and you wanted something, like a toy. Now, let's say this thing you wanted it was an Xbox One, the first Xbox. When you were younger, you probably thought that this thing would bring you lots of happiness. You had dreams about it, you talked about it, and you begged your parents to buy it for you. If you were lucky, perhaps your parents did give in and they bought you the Xbox.

For the first few weeks or so, you were ecstatic. You were very happy, and you had heaps of joy as you played this thing. You played it until the gimmick wore off. What naturally happened is you started growing tired of it, so the happiness faded, and you wanted something more. You wanted something else to rekindle that excitement. So, the next thing you go for is maybe the Xbox 360, or a new bike, or maybe a new laptop, and so begins the cycle. Let me tell you a quick story that will help you internalize this point.

A few years ago, I wanted a new laptop. I dreamt about. I was obsessed with the idea, and I saved money from time to time, convincing myself that when I got this laptop, I would be happy. I'd be completely content. So, I got the laptop, and I was right! I was happy and I was completely content for a week, maybe. Then after a week, I got bored of the laptop and I wanted something better. This is the hedonic treadmill. My happiness level increased, but then it went back to the default level of happiness.

Now, this cycle doesn't end during childhood. It continues to adulthood. We are always looking for new job positions, new cars, new material things, new positions, or all of the above.

But at the end of the day, we end up going back to a base level of happiness. Why are we never able to truly be content or fulfilled? Because there is always something else. It never ends.

If you were to lose your house right now and start living on the streets, of course you might be depressed to begin with. You might actually be suicidal for a while, but after a few months, maybe a year or two, your base level of happiness goes back to where it was. You adapt to the situation.

If you were to become a multimillionaire right now, you'd be pretty happy and you'd have a lot of time to enjoy yourself, but after a few years, once again, your base level of happiness returns to its normal level. This is why people are so surprised when they see celebrities that get depressed or commit suicide. This is what people don't understand about the hedonic adaptation. Material things don't matter.

After a while, things change, but happiness comes from within and it comes from paying attention to the present moment and enjoying it without really needing anything more. Once again, this doesn't necessarily mean that you shouldn't aspire for great things, but it means that you should be able to take some time to reflect, sit down, and enjoy the present moment.

Think of ways that this has happened in your life, and I promise you will find some resemblance to this situation. Then, remind yourself that you can stop looking for external things to increase your level of happiness, because happiness comes from within.

I urge you to understand that happiness resides within yourself. You have happiness inside of your body. Just realize that, and you will be joyful, I promise.

How Happiness Feels to A Stoic

I'm going to guess that you've already read multiple articles and have gone through multiple books about happiness, and yet your happiness hasn't multiplied. Why is that? Listening and reading aren't the same as doing.

All behavior, and all changes, must be trained. Stoics didn't write their material solely to be read. They created practical exercises in order to train your mind to respond properly to life so that you could live it well. Stoicism isn't concerned with difficult sayings and philosophies.

Its focus is on helping us overcome harmful feelings and work on the things that can be changed.

Simply put, here are the Stoics most important exercises for happiness:

Get Rid of Your Obstacles

This exercise is very powerful, because if you can properly fight your obstacles and get rid of them, you can become happy. Every bad becomes a potential source of good to the stoic. Everything is an opportunity.

For example, situations where your hard work is underpaid or the demise or loss of a loved one occurs are not considered opportunities, generally. In fact, they can make you weak because they are obstacles. What do the stoic do? They believe there is a lesson to be learned in each and every experience we have in life, and that every obstacle that comes our way leads to more growth.

Rather than sulking or complaining, stoics ask themselves, "What have I learned from this experience?" and "How have I become a better person?" These are empowering questions. Most of us are not completely immune to external events or the bad things that happen to us.

These result in bad feelings within us. However, recognizing that our lives still go on and we can't pity our situations is an outlook that can give us a completely different way of living. More importantly, this outlook can make us strong in adverse situations.

Is This Within My Control?

One of the most important practices in stoic philosophy is differentiating between what we can change and what we can't. Let's say a flight was delayed because of the weather, and no amount of arguing with the airline representative will end the bad weather. In another example, physically we may be taller or shorter than we want, but no amount of wishing will change that. What's important to realize is the time spent mulling over these unchangeable situations is often wasted. Don't fight the battles you can't win. When you realize that you can't control certain things, you feel happier.

Appreciate the Present

Chasing future happiness is self-defeating. We can find happiness by accepting the present. If you refuse to accept your reality and always hope that you deserve a better future, this can result in robbing yourselves and present happiness. By seeing happiness as an outcome of some future achievements such as getting a certain job, more money, or finding a spouse, we start to lose sight of what we already have as our happiness right in this very moment. And even worse the plans for the future happiness do not go as desired. We will grow depressed similar to chasing future happiness. The Stoics believe that developing a constant desire for one thing after another can be a reason to unhappiness. So, they implanted the idea of accepting and gratifying things that are already there. By doing so, you can find ultimate satisfaction in whatever you have.

How to be Happy Being a Stoic Using the Stoic Triangle Eudaimonia

The main mantra of stoicism is eudaimonia. This phenomenon explains how to be happy with your higher self or how to stay calm on the inside. In other words, this part of the happiness triangle can also be explained by supreme happiness. How to achieve this? Just be good to your inner domain and follow three famous principles of stoic happiness triangle, which are explained as follows:

1. Live with Areté - To do this, you have to align your innermost beliefs (good ones) with your actions. Just become the best version of yourself and express yourself a lot.

2. Focus on the controllable things - The most prominent teaching of stoicism is to focus on what you can control rather than what is not in your control. Accept whatever is happening around you, whether it is good or bad, but have control over your actions and your thoughts.

3. Be responsible - Take responsibility for your life. External events can't make you happy or miserable. It's solely up to you how to react in different situations. If you can become responsible about how you choose to stay calm despite the external happenings, you are on your way to being extremely happy.

Chapter 5:
Applying Stoicism: The Struggle for Self-Sufficiency

N umerous persons today face an unforgiving adventure to turn out to be financially independent. For various entry-level positions in multiple fields, hindrances may incorporate a prerequisite for earlier work understanding, different degrees, or a mix of both.

As it is hard to acquire a section level position without previous work experience, additional education requests higher financial risks for uncertain returns.

Some might almost certainly bear the cost of more education without taking on debt, to a great extent, leaving time and exertion as outstanding expenses. For other people, outside money related help or graduating with generous obligation is fundamental.

Depending on the desired field, the propelled degree will not always be an advantage; the degree may instead spot one's odds for consideration on even ground with other applicants. For a significant advantage, familiar obstacles should be survived, multiplying the costs accordingly. Some may likewise have an edge in the type of social contacts, networks, or support trading.

Every individual's experience with this cycle will shift depending on many interweaving events. It likely could be that the period finishes as sought after, and a private ground the sought-for position. An individual may decide not to face the period by any means, deeming the risked investment too significant without some guarantee of future stability.

If an individual believes another person (for example, another applicant or business) represents a barrier or intends to something great, they are more likely to carry on in ways that are counter-intuitive to their goal.

For instance, they may make a special effort to pick words that seem learned or change their non-verbal communication to seem exceptionally confident.

They might be bound to adorn their resume, exaggerate their work understanding, or overstate individual stories during meetings. In the event that they're offered a position, they should consistently work to keep up any intentional deceptions created from the outset.

The miscellaneous risks of pursuing a propelled degree are regularly not the primary considerations in play:

As it is necessary for businesses (at least in the United States) to be obscure in their reasoning for turning down an applicant, the individual may take it upon themselves to fill in the spaces: "Possibly I just don't have what it takes." "I merited that way more than whoever got it!" "I gave 110% – it ought to have been sufficient." "Those individuals don't realize who is passing up beside them, and they would be sober while they figure out."

To many, a career represents something great because of the material benefits thought to go with them. A feeling of ownership is steadily projected onto potential employment propositions in the act of following it intently. If the position is not offered, it is accordingly considered these benefits are "lost."

The Stoics suggest that much valuing external things is a mistake and a disservice to us, given our capacity for reason and choice – a capability unique to our species. Investing worth and effort in decisions that are consistent with our distinctive nature as social and rational animals is held to be the primary right path to becoming upbeat; notably, happiness that is independent of the external obstacles interfering with financial self-sufficiency:

Evacuate want for void popularity, the notoriety of a savant, or to have carried on with as long as you can remember as a thinker. An incredible arrangement contradicts it. Dispose of worry for how others see you and be substance to carry on with a mind-blowing rest without diversion, coordinated by your inclination.

You have encountered numerous wanderings without discovering bliss; not in syllogisms, nor riches, nor notoriety, not delight, nor anyplace. Where is it at that point? In completing a man's, the same old thing. What to do? Pursue your rules that identify with fortunate or unfortunate with the conviction that there is no good thing for man that does not make him simply, mild, masculine and free and that there is nothing awful that does not do the opposite.

People need to survive as other animals do physically, but little more is required past the basics: a couple of suppers daily, water, clothing, and shelter. Anything additional is sought after by choice; a choice made in the interest of this basic impulse.

The moment, notwithstanding, that we begin depending on the presence of unusual things or fear their nonappearance is the moment we've surrendered control of ourselves to the persons that might manipulate them.

Different things are merchandise by sentiment, "points of interest," "liked" things. Assets, not parts of we, they loan no man cause to tuft himself. Give us a chance to utilize these things, yet not flaunt them. Barely any men have been permitted to drop thriving delicately, the rest all fall together with their assets and are weighted somewhere around these very things which once lifted up them.

Utilize breaking points and cheapness since permit ousts is claim bounty. That which has no restriction has never allowed motivation as far as possible for it. Numerous an extraordinary power has tumbled to extravagance and been obliterated; overabundance has destroyed what was won by ideals. Our weapon of protection is our capacity to acknowledge what befalls us.

Striving to act in light of the dichotomy between what is or is not in our control is crucial to the eventual transformation of our everyday thought process – a thought procedure that may otherwise be filled continuously with resentment, anxiety, fear, and hyper-competitiveness with others.

It is not a guarantee, as mentioned because our exercise of choice alone is entirely within our control, but it stops to be the ultimate objective on the path to becoming practicing Stoics:

Your feelings of dread are inert and your wants vain. Try not to look for beneficial things outside of yourself, yet inside, or you won't discover them. When you think things are going seriously recall you are being prepared for instance to other men. When you are delegated to such a job it isn't for you to think about where or in what organization you are or what others state about you, yet to spend your endeavors complying with the directions of Zeus (Nature).

In the event that you remember these considerations you will never need for one to comfort and support you. Disrespect does not originate from not having enough to eat, however, from not having enough right motivation to verify you from dread and torment.

When you are free from dread and torment you are free from every single natural oppression. Make no presentation of your office by blowing up yourself yet substantiate yourself by direct. Be content, however none watch you, to live in obvious wellbeing and joy.

How Can Stoicism Help Me?

We can talk all day about the intangible benefits of living Stoically, but we are first and foremost selfish beings – eager to help ourselves and interested in the tangible benefits to ourselves. This is not a point of shame. It makes sense to wonder how Stoicism can help you and to take into account what you are getting out of it. Stoicism, after all, asks a great deal of adherents, and if you follow Stoic philosophy to the tee, you probably have to make drastic changes to your lifestyle.

So, how can Stoicism help me?

To answer this question, we need to think about the problems that people are facing en masse. What are the ills and ailments that have become endemic to modern society? Even a cursory look at statistics will tell you that mental illness is on the rise. 20% of adults experience mental illness at some level, and 4% experience serious mental illness. There is sometimes no substitute for medical intervention, but if you feel like you could use a minor leg-up with regard to your mental health, Stoicism can offer some guidance.

Think about anxiety for a moment. What is it? It is worrying about the future, worrying that something negative is going to happen, that harm and danger are imminent. Anxiety can sometimes cripple, sending people down a rabbit hole where nothing that they do is ever right. In Stoic philosophy, though, anxiety would be just one more feeling, something to acknowledge, something to move on from.

Similarly, depression in its major chemical forms may require medication, but for its minor forms, a mental shift may be sufficient. Stoic philosophy, which teaches us to focus on living virtuously and to maintain calm, reminds us of the transience of all our emotions, and if we study Stoicism vigorously, we may end up putting our feelings of anger, sadness, guilt, and regret into contexts where they have less power over us.

In all areas of your life, you would do well to maintain calm and contextualize your emotions – as Stoic philosophers would urge you to do. You set a goal for yourself, envisioning how you will feel when you reach your goal and devising a plan to get from here to there, and pursuing that goal, you want to remember that no matter what happens to you, everything will work out. Committed as you are to reach your goal, you remain detached from it to an extent, which makes composure possible even in the most strenuous circumstances.

Your work, your education, your relationships: you know that you would be better off leaving emotions mostly out of these realms, thinking reasonably and logically, considering others' points of view from a position of clarity. Like a boat in the middle of a tempest, you are much less likely to sink if your boards and your sails are all pointing in the proper directions, sturdy at their core and not shifting every way the waves push them.

All of this comes down to peace. Fight for it, hope for it, work for it – peace is more often than not something that you need to find inside yourself. Reigning during the Pax Romana, Marcus Aurelius nonetheless oversaw multiple military conflicts, witnessing countless deaths, not only of his enemies but of his own comrades. It was not the battles that defined him, though.

Success, achievement, clarity, virtue – these are the words that we associate with Emperor Aurelius, to whom academics have referred adoringly as "the Philosopher" over the last two millennia. Beset on all sides, he made a name for himself by remaining unbothered and holding onto his poise despite all else. You too can make a name for yourself, living the good life, the virtuous life, the Stoic life – living the way that Stoics from Zeno on down would have liked.

Chapter 6: Meditation

So far, we have considered the importance of accepting change and the hell we put ourselves through when we fight with reality (change).

We have learned that we get frustrated when a change occurs differently from what we expected. But the truth is, our discomfort and distress don't come from the change but from us. We get distressed when we hold on to a belief that doesn't correlate with our immediate experience. And, instead of looking at things critically, we meet the change/circumstance with aggression, when we can simply change how we think about the experience.

This is the summary of the Stoic philosophy—developing a rigid spirit not moved by external circumstances.

"Live through life in the best way you can. The power to do so is in a man's own soul if he is indifferent to things indifferent. And he will be indifferent if he looked at these things both as a whole and analyzed into their parts and remembers that none of them imposes a judgment of itself or forces itself on us. The things themselves are inert."

—Marcus Aurelius, Meditations

The moment we come to terms with the fact that circumstances, changes, and events are all neutral, and that there is no special meaning to events in life except that which we ascribe, then we stop being victims of circumstance. Our joy and happiness are no longer tied to the happening around us; we are free!

The simple concept of Stoicism can be a helpful starting point for having our personal code of conduct/core values. We make ourselves realize what is and isn't within our control, persistently working towards what we can accept and learning to accept what is out of our control.

Let us consider the example of an everyday act of driving.

Every blessed day, we drive on the road, having similar road conditions with other road users. We hold on to the belief that other road users should drive properly and appropriately, just like we would. However, when we fall short of our expectations, we lose it. We fume, "people just suck at driving!" Due to the false mental image we have, we have an awful emotional response to things beyond our control, intentionally making ourselves sad.

The moment we learn and know how to accept changes as they come, we are no longer programmed to react and respond to circumstances.

Below are some extracts from meditations that further drive the point that we can live a happy, fulfilled, joyous, and full life, by learning to accept what we can and cannot change.

Accepting What Is

"Don't seek for everything to happen as you wish it would, but rather wish that everything happens as it actually will—then, your life will flow well."

—Epictetus, Enchiridion

When something happens to us, which can we easily change? Our opinion of the event or the event itself?

I am pretty sure you know the answer. This is one of the reasons we have to change our attitude. Accept what has happened and avoid wasting emotions, thinking it didn't happen. The Stoics call this the "art of acquiescence."

Rather than fighting or questioning what happened, accept it. It also doesn't stop at acceptance; we have to enjoy the process as it happens— the change process. I am pretty sure Thomas Edison wouldn't have had the idea of the light bulb had he detested the event of his burning lab.

We save ourselves from disappointment, heartache, and negative emotions when we subtly wish for what has happened to happen. This ensures that nothing happens against our will.

When we love and enjoy the process of the event, we set ourselves up for joy and happiness.

Binding Our Wishes on What Will Be

I will explain this meditation with the story of General Dwight D. Eisenhower. On the night before the invasion of Normandy, he wrote to his wife and told her, "We have tried all in our capacity—the troops are prepared, and everyone has done their best. The outcome lies with the gods." General Dwight D. Eisenhower affirmed that although he and his troops had done all that was humanly possible, what would happen would happen. And, from the writings of Epictetus, he was prepared to bear what was coming.

History also had it that General Eisenhower had another letter prepared to be released should the invasion have failed. If the failure was what God/fate/luck or whatever had planned, he was ready. This story has a terrific lesson for us all. General Dwight D. Eisenhower can be said to be the leader of one of the most powerful, fearless, and brave battalions. Yet, on the night of one of the most epic battles, he was humble and knowledgeable enough to admit that the outcome was not in his hands, but in the hands of something or someone way bigger than him.

Let this guide us in our entire life's endeavor. King Solomon, one of the wisest Kings the Earth has ever seen, had many things to say in this regard:

"The horse is prepared for the day of the battle, but safety is of the Lord."

—Proverbs 21:31

In other words, no matter how confident we feel that we are ready/prepared for something, we have no final say concerning the ultimate outcome.

Not Good, Not Bad

People are suspicious of change, and by default, we are programmed to perceive change as a threat. If we have a group of five monkeys, and we introduce a new monkey into the cage, the new one is obviously a threat. We are, by default, programmed to dislike change or to be suspicious of change.

As a result, when we hear people say, "Change is good," it is a conscious effort to reassure themselves of others.

Let us come to the Stoic philosophy now. Stoicism teaches us to let go of those labels. There is nothing awful in change; neither is the status quo the best. Remember, we are what we make of it—neither good nor bad.

A Higher Power

I will explain this quote with the twelve-step program that is used in nursing addicts back to health. It is common for many addicts to have issues with the second step—acknowledging a higher power. Addicts just do not like hearing this.

They attribute this to various reasons, such as being an atheist or their hatred for religion. With time, however, many come to terms with the fact that it is their addiction getting in the way again—a sign of self-absorption. Yet, what many addicts fail to realize is that a higher power/authority is needed to help in their total restoration. The other steps require the addict to let go, yet it (the letting go process) has less to do with the 'higher power' than the other steps.

The further steps involve harmonizing with the universe and releasing the erroneous idea that we are in the driving seat. This wisdom, without a doubt, is applicable to us all.

The idea is simple—even if we are an atheist, we are not asked to believe in a god. Rather, let go of the idea that we are in control. The moment this realization sinks in, we will enjoy an easy and happy life.

Actors in a Play

History revealed to us that it was not in Marcus Aurelius' plan to become an emperor. He was neither a politician that was interested in politics nor a true heir. Deductions from his letters revealed that he longed to be a philosopher.

However, the then emperor, Hadrian, and the knowledgeable elites in Rome saw potential in Marcus. He was adopted, prepared for power, and groomed for the throne because they knew he had the capacity. Epictetus, on the other hand, was a slave for a very long time and was even harassed due to his teachings. Marcus and Epictetus performed wonderfully with their assigned roles.

Our role in life can be chosen randomly, just as if we're rolling dice. Some are lucky to be born with a silver spoon while others don't get that privilege. And yet there are times when the playing ground is level for all.

Part of the teachings of the Stoics reminds us that all that happens through the course of human life, wherever we find ourselves, we are not to grumble. Rather, we need to try all we can to accept, love, and fulfill it.

Yes, there is still room for ambition. The stage of life we are acting out is filled with stories in little parts, which later become beautiful roles that are seen in various manifestations in our lives. However, this cannot happen without acceptance, love, and the zeal to joyfully perform excellently at our roles.

Everything is Change

It is not possible to step in the same river twice—Marcus Aurelius borrowed this powerful metaphor from Heraclitus. This is because, with time, the river changes (in composition, quality, color), likewise does the man.

The only thing constant about life is change, since it changes constantly. When we are upset by change or circumstances, we wrongly assume that the change will last.

Blaming ourselves or wishing things were different is an attempt to catch the wind. Besides, we give ourselves the false impression that we have a choice in the matter. Rather, we should come to terms with the fact that change is constant; embrace it and love it.

Foundations of a Successful Stoic Meditation

Meditation is not about a simple task of positioning yourself comfortably on your mat with your eyes closed- like what we see on TV on in magazines. There's a lot more that goes into the process than you may have initially realized. There are a few things you need to know before you begin your meditation journey. Firstly, meditation is a very personal thing and an entirely unique experience for different people. Secondly, while it is a personal experience, there are still some fundamentals which you can rely on to help you achieve a successful meditation session.

Essential Keys to Helping You Meditate Successfully

These essentials are not too complicated or restrictive. If you're ready to begin your successful meditation journey, here are five fundamental steps you can keep in mind to achieve optimum success during your sessions:

1.Get rid of any expectations – Did you decide to begin meditation expecting to get something specific out of each session? If you did, you're going to need to learn to let that go. Meditation sessions are different, some days will be easier than others, some days will seem longer than others. If you go into it with expectations in mind, you're only setting yourself up for disappointment if things don't go your way.

So, let go of any expectations and approach each session with an open mind and the possibility that anything can happen, come what you will, just go with it without resistance.

2.Set the right environment – Find a space that is conducive to meditation. Your environment should not only be one that is set-up to infuse you with feelings of calm and relaxation, a space that you look forward to spending time in, but it must also be a space that is quiet, free of noise, clutter, bright lights, devices and anything else which could prove to be a distraction. Your environment should promote a feeling of peace and serenity, somewhere you can't wait to rush home to and spend some time in, that way you will look forward to each session and immerse yourself completely in the experience for optimum success.

3.Be mindful throughout the day – One of the purposes that meditation is there to bring is a greater state of mindfulness, teaching you to pay greater attention to your surroundings and be conscious about your actions and your feelings. Being in a state of mindfulness doesn't have to stop the minute your timer goes off to signal meditation time is over.

Instead, bring mindfulness with you every moment you're awake and as you go about your daily routine. No matter what task you may be handling at the moment, do it with mindfulness and focus. In other words, give each task your complete attention. This will help you sharpen your focus and you will see what a difference this makes when you undergo your meditation sessions.

How to Build a Habit of Regularly Practicing Meditation

Meditation works the same way as any other habit or practice or even skill that you want to cultivate. You need to have been regularly practicing meditation before you can accomplish a state of deep meditation, which is taking it to the next level.

The best way to do that is to make it a habit of practicing meditation every day if possible, but at least several times in a week. Meditation needs to be a part of your life the way eating a meal is. It has to be something that you want to do every day without fail. If you've been struggling to develop the habit, try the following methods to help you along the way:

How to Discipline Yourself to Spend at Least 30 Mins a Day on Meditation

You can start small of course, but at least 30 minutes a day is what you eventually want to work your way up to because that's going to be part of the 4-week plan. The best way to start disciplining yourself to do this is simple – you need to reflect on why this is important to you. Why did you decide to take up meditating in the first place? What did you hope to accomplish through this practice?

1.Finding your 'why' is how you find the drive to keep going and to stick to what you set out to do. Without a reason, you're going to flounder and eventually give up altogether, because there's nothing pushing you to keep going. Remind yourself of why you decided to make a commitment to do this, write it down on a post-it and stick it all over your house and workspace if it helps to remind you to keep going.

2.Start small with just 2 – 30 minutes is what you want to eventually work up to. If you're just starting out, don't sweat it, just start small and work your way up from there. Starting with 2 minutes each day is more than good enough to get the ball rolling and once it becomes a habit, it'll be easier for you to go for long periods without even noticing it.

3.Work with others – Joining a friend or a group of people who are on the same meditation goal path as you are can go a long way in helping you build a habit of making this a regular practice. Knowing that you're not alone on this journey can prove to be a tremendous form of support as well as establish a sense of belonging.

Plus, having the company makes the activity more enjoyable, especially if you're the sociable type who likes being around others.

4.Remember you're doing this for yourself – When is the last time you did anything for yourself? Taken the time out to focus on you and what you need? We get so busy and caught up with everything going on in our lives it's easy to let our own needs slide or just be completely forgotten altogether. But you owe it to yourself to take care of yourself in the best possible way.

You're doing this for yourself, and no one else. You're doing this so you can reap all the benefits meditation has to offer you, and no one else. You owe it to yourself to step back each day from everything that is consuming you and spend at that recuperating and recharging yourself.

5.Let go of the judgements – If you're going to constantly berate yourself throughout whenever you think you're not performing as you should, meditation is not going to be a very pleasant experience for you, nor is it going to be beneficial in any way. Meditation is about letting go of the things that hold you down emotionally and mentally, and this includes letting go of your need to be perfect all the time. Don't be too hard on yourself whenever you stumble along the way, it's how you learn to get better and be better. Instead of fixating on how you think your meditation session should go, just let go and immerse yourself in the experience, no matter what may unfold.

6.Pick a consistent time – Understandably, your schedule is likely to be different each day. To develop the meditation habit, try and assess your regular pattern throughout the week. Compare that to a couple of weeks and see if there are any drastic changes or movements to your scheduled times. And from there, pick a time of day which you think would work best every day of the week, every week. It doesn't have to be a specific time per se, just a general one like deciding you will meditate in the morning before breakfast, or in the afternoon, or during your lunch hour, or even at the end of the day before you go to bed. Sticking to a regular time frame each day will help you develop the habit much easier.

Chapter 7:
Common Misconceptions of Stoicism

T he Stoic tradition is one of only a few ancient philosophies that have stood the test of time. While other traditions faded and became extinct, Stoicism has maintained a steady following, becoming increasingly popular during times of political and social turmoil. One of the downsides of this, however, is that the Stoic image has become more and more misconstrued over time. Common misinterpretations of Stoic ideals have paved the way for a perception of the average Stoic that is about as far off the mark as you can possibly get. Even worse, such misconceptions have led to the term 'Stoic' being adopted into the pop-culture vernacular to indicate a mindset that isn't entirely Stoic at all. The end result is that while many people recognize the term 'Stoic,' and even have a fair idea as to what the term means, very few people actually understand the true nature of Stoicism. It is therefore essential that some of these common misconceptions of Stoicism be cleared up once and for all.

Stoics are Ascetic

The first misconception to address is that Stoics are ascetic. While not the most common misconception, this idea is still one that is widely believed. The reason behind this confusion is that several Ancient Greek philosophies were in fact ascetic in nature. Cynicism, for example, was a tradition that flourished at the exact same time as Stoicism, and it was one that promoted a very ascetic way of life. One theory suggests that stories regarding the ascetic traditions of India made their way to the Classical World, influencing such great minds as Socrates, Diogenes and Antisthenes—traditionally recognized as the founder of Cynicism. Additionally, some philosophers practiced an ascetic way of life even when their doctrines didn't demand it of their followers. Therefore, an image of austerity and self-deprivation follows just about every Ancient Greek philosophy, including that of Stoicism.

While the Stoic philosophy does involve a great deal of discipline, especially regarding desire and action, it does not encourage outright asceticism. In fact, the Discipline of Desire is perhaps Zeno's answer to the ascetic issue. Once a student of Cynicism, Zeno turned to his own path due to misgivings that he had about the tradition. A common belief is that he wasn't happy with the extreme aspects of the philosophy, including the promotion of an ascetic lifestyle. Although Zeno embraced the Cynics' belief in nature as a guiding force, he felt that they missed the point in other ways. Stoicism wasn't about depriving oneself of pleasure or happiness, rather it was about ensuring that an individual's desires would lead to true happiness, not the shallow and unfulfilling happiness that came from greed, folly and the mindless pursuit of pleasure. This is where the three disciplines came into play. Additionally, the concept of moderation in all things dispels any notion that asceticism has a role in the Stoic tradition.

It is also worth noting that Zeno promoted the idea that the Stoic practitioner should take the time to appreciate the things they have in their life. Rather than getting rid of everything, it was advised that one should get rid of those things that didn't actually bring pleasure, thereby enjoying those things that did. Ultimately, while Stoicism teaches the dangers of materialism it doesn't advocate a complete break from having possessions. Instead, much like the minimalist tradition of today, Stoicism advocates the idea that less is more. Taking pleasure in the simple things in life is the true Stoic ideal. Therefore, any image of Zeno walking around without any possessions whatsoever is largely exaggerated, missing the true essence of Stoic values completely. While we don't know the extent of what Zeno did or did not possess, one thing we can be sure of is that he appreciated anything he did have.

Stoics are Emotionless

Another common misconception of Stoicism is that Stoics are emotionless. This is probably the most common of all Stoic misconceptions in circulation today. Again, this mistakes the idea of discipline for that of eradication. While Stoicism does teach that the individual should be in total control of their emotions it does not suggest that emotions should be eliminated altogether. Just as desire should be regulated and not eliminated, so too, emotions should be kept in check and not surgically removed. Unfortunately, the image of the ascetic Greek philosopher engenders the idea of an emotionless, logic-obsessed mindset. And that is where this misconception comes from.

One of the most common embodiments of this erroneous idea is Mr. Spock from Star Trek. The cold and calculating, completely unemotional personality are a direct reflection of the idea of Stoicism at the time the show was produced. Even worse, the term 'Stoic' has come to mean facing adverse conditions with a cold and unemotional disposition. While it is true that Zeno advised against allowing emotions to control a person, it is wholly untrue that he ever intended a person to become completely detached from their emotions. The idea of being unemotional ignores the Stoic belief that nature is inherently perfect. Zeno and the early Stoics marveled at nature, believing that it was the true, unadulterated essence of the Universe itself. Anyone who observes nature will notice that animals are very emotional, demonstrating everything from anger to joy and even love. Therefore, emotions themselves should be embraced, not rejected.

The true essence of the Stoic view of emotions is that they need to be controlled. Since uncontrolled emotions could lead to actions that cause distress and suffering, it is critical to not let one's emotions run amok. This is where the Discipline of Action comes into play. Rather than envisioning a Stoic as a person without emotion, it would be more accurate to envision a Stoic as one who experiences an emotional response to a stimulus, just like a normal person, but who then takes the time to bring that response under control, thereby preventing it from clouding their judgment. Counting to ten before taking action is perhaps one of the most Stoic practices in use today. And it embodies the place for emotions within the Stoic practitioner. After all, the Stoic concept of Apatheia isn't a lack of emotion, rather it is a lack of unbridled emotion. Therefore, Mr. Spock may be many things, but Stoic isn't one of them.

Stoics Prefer Hardship

Finally, there is the misconception that Stoics prefer hardship. This idea is the byproduct of the previous misconceptions regarding the ascetic and unemotional Stoic. After all, anyone who chooses to reject all possessions and cut off all emotion must prefer hardship to comfort or pleasure. While this might be true for someone matching that description, the fact of the matter is that it is not true for the practicing Stoic. Therefore, this is a matter of conjecture based entirely on misinformation. The reality is that although Stoics are perhaps better prepared for hardship, they don't prefer them. Instead, the average Stoic would rather that things went well, just like any other reasonable person.

The notion that Stoics prefer hardship is also founded in a misunderstanding of the Stoic principle of embracing hardship. This principle encourages a Stoic practitioner to face hardship with courage rather than with disdain or even worse, trying to escape hardship altogether. Embracing hardship merely means that you should accept it when it comes, nothing more. By embracing it, you don't allow it to control your life, nor do you take it personally. Instead, you simply take hardship in your stride knowing that it will pass in due course. This incorporates the Stoic idea of impermanence as well. Thus, embracing hardship isn't about desiring hardship, rather it is about recognizing that things are never as bad as they seem.

Another reason why Zeno encouraged the Stoic practitioner to embrace hardship was so that they would better appreciate it when things went well. In other words, when an individual embraces the bad times in life, they are better able to appreciate and relish in the good times. Nowhere does Zeno encourage a person to run from good times. He only ever suggested that you shouldn't run from the bad times. By facing both bad times and good with a steady heart and a clear mind you will be in constant control of your life, no matter what the circumstances may be.

Myths And Misconceptions

If you have never heard of Stoicism the philosophy, you have likely come across stoicism (small s) in your life. In modern English, the word stoic is used to describe people who remain self-possessed in the face of adversity. While often admirable, to be "stoic" has the potential to become unhealthy. If you merely repress emotions, holding back inner turmoil, but never truly deal with those internal issues, the outcome can be devastating. This is not Stoicism with a capital S. Even the ancient Stoics dealt with this mischaracterization of their philosophy; their critics saw it as a cold thing. And yet the Stoics insisted that no one should aim to be an unfeeling statue. Developing a virtuous life actually leads to a rich emotional life, one in which you are skillful with those emotions—cultivating the positive, while quickly overcoming the negative.

Another misconception is passivity. Stoicism says you can thrive in any situation; it teaches acceptance of the world as it is. This can be misinterpreted as apathy. "Why change," they say, "if one can be happy even in the worst of life's storms?"

It may seem paradoxical, but Stoic acceptance actually gives you the strength to overcome challenges. Passivity arises more often from fear than from acceptance. When a rude person makes aggressive demands, how often do you just give in, worrying that standing up for yourself would make matters worse? The Stoic accepts that the person in front of them is being hostile, but they can choose how to respond. If the belligerent person's demands are unjust, the Stoic works for justice. Stoicism teaches you to be clear-eyed so you can make the best possible choices. As you learn to trust your capacity to tackle trials, inaction and indecision stop being obstacles. When you direct your attention toward what you can control, your actions become well-aimed and effective.

Before we look in depth at the tools Stoicism provides, let's look briefly at where these ideas began.

MODERN STOICISM

"I do not bind myself to some particular one of the Stoic teachers. I too have a right to form an opinion."

—Seneca, On the Happy Life

Modern Stoicism focuses heavily on ethics. The ancient Stoics divided their schooling into three broad topics: physics, logic, and ethics. While there is intellectual value in reading Stoic thoughts on physics and logic, most Stoics want to get to the part that helps them thrive. The Stoic approach to living has captured our attention. In fact, a modern therapeutic practice, Cognitive Behavioral Therapy (CBT), was influenced by Stoic writings. Much of its approach to emotional life and many of its practices align with Stoicism. CBT helps people think in a healthier way but does not provide a road map to a flourishing life. The Stoic philosophy uses similar mental practices but combines them with a set of values that can guide you toward your best self. It's that coupling of mental clarity with a sense of purpose that has attracted so many to Stoicism.

Modern Stoicism also looks at our relationship with the universe differently. Many ancient Stoics were pious pantheists who perceived the universe as a benevolent god known as Zeus. Modern practice embraces a more secular point of view. If you are not religious, Stoicism retains all its usefulness. If you are religious and choose to adopt Stoicism, the philosophy meshes better if its theology is left behind.

ABOUT PANTHEISTS

People often refer to the ancient Stoics as pantheists. This is a bit anachronistic, as pantheism is a modern conception—the term itself did not arise until 1697 CE. That said, Stoic theology does fit the pantheist definition of either believing that god is the universe or that the universe is a manifestation of god.

Most early Stoics believed that the entire universe was interconnected as one being, a single organism they called Zeus, who is synonymous with Nature and Reason.

In modern times, Stoic practice is more personalized than in the past. It's unlikely that you will live at a Stoic school like Epictetus's students did. This does not mean you have to be lonely! There are vibrant online communities dedicated to Stoicism and a growing number of groups all over the world who meet face-to-face to discuss the philosophy. There are even conferences for practical Stoicism. I aim to leave you with a solid foundation so you can thrive on your own, but there's a growing world out there for you to participate in.

Stoicism is here for anyone: It says that all human beings are family and each of us are worthy of a loving respect. Stoicism proclaims that all people are capable of living lives of wisdom. Even in ancient times the philosophy reached a diverse range of people. As already mentioned, the Stoic teacher Epictetus began life as a slave, while the practitioner Marcus Aurelius led an empire; Stoicism has been inclusive since its origin. Although it developed in societies that were highly patriarchal, Stoic writings clearly put forth that women are moral equals who deserve to be trained in philosophy. Even so, among the old Stoics we primarily find men—often affluent ones—and they were sometimes locked into the thinking of their times. Thankfully, we are not bound by

Greek and Roman customs. Our modern community lives up to the best of Stoic thought and contains a diverse, vibrant, and growing population.

REFLECTION

When you are ready to begin some undertaking, remind yourself what the nature of that undertaking is. If you are going out of the house to bathe, put before your mind what happens at a public bath—those who splash you with water, those who jostle against you, those who vilify you and rob you. You will set about your undertaking more securely if before beginning you say to yourself, "I want to take a bath, and, at the same time, to keep my moral purpose in harmony with nature." And do this for every undertaking.

For if anything happens to hinder you in your bathing, you will be ready to say, "Oh, well, this was not the only thing that I wanted, but I wanted also to keep my moral purpose in harmony with nature; and I will not do that if I am annoyed at what is going on."

—EPICTETUS, ENCHIRIDION 4

Continuous Stoic practice reshapes your moral character. The fundamental focus of Stoicism involves that character—your best self—because this is wholly within your control. The next time you do anything, remind yourself, "I want to do this task, and, at the same time, I want to protect my harmony."

Ask yourself:

•In the task before me, what challenges could arise?

•In confronting those challenges, how can I be my best self and remain in harmony with life?

WHY STOICISM?

You have the capacity to thrive. The Stoic goal is eudaimonia, a flourishing life. With focused practice, you can cultivate a life that is serene, joyful, and enthusiastic, even in the face of great challenges. You will find yourself less angry, anxious, and lonely as your Stoic mind-set makes negative emotions less likely to take root.

I work as a health and safety instructor. Each morning, I drive to a different business in Oregon to train a group of people I've never met. My morning commute can range from 15 minutes to three hours. The groups I meet might be attentive and inquisitive or they may be sneaking looks at their phones or obviously frustrated that they have to attend my training. On top of this, there may be personal issues in my own life that could distract me from giving my best presentation. I begin my day with a Stoic meditation that reminds me I am capable of facing any obstacle I meet. I have mental tools like the Dichotomy of Control, which helps me focus on those things I have the ability to change. Stoicism has given me the Festival Mind-set, in which every crowd becomes a party, and which helps me enjoy what others may find frustrating. At night, I do an Evening Review, which allows me to openly evaluate myself and leads me to improve myself day by day. Soon, you will have these same tools and much more. With practice, you'll gain the flourishing life that Stoicism promises.

Before we move forward, take a moment to think about how I've described the Stoic life. It's:

• flourishing

• in good flow

• in harmony with nature

Right now, what do these phrases mean to you? If you were to attain the goal of living a flourishing life in harmony with nature, what would that look like? What steps could you take today to bring yourself closer to this vision?

STOICISM FOR EVERYONE

How you define a "good flow of life" is unique to you. The challenges you face in life are likely wildly different from my challenges. Thankfully, each of us can apply the tools of Stoicism for our own particular purposes. For example, I watched my wife use the philosophy during a difficult pregnancy. Doctors cautioned us throughout that time that our daughter may not survive, and that Christy's life was at risk as well.

Despite an uncertain future, she focused on the present, which let her find joy in the moment. She placed her attention on her thoughts and opinions, the things she controlled, which kept her from being overwhelmed by life's anxieties. The Stoic mind-set provided peace amid turmoil. Practitioners use the philosophy to show up fully in relationships, to find fulfillment in work (often in spite of that work), and to manage day-to-day struggles. I've also met Stoics who use the philosophy to manage addiction, chronic pain, or, like myself, emotional issues. Whatever challenges will come your way, Stoicism provides a means of thriving as you face them.

In order to access all these benefits, you will need to look at yourself clearly, be open to exploring the unique perspective that Stoicism offers and be willing to practice diligently. As Musonius Rufus, a Roman Stoic teacher, said, "Practicing each virtue always must follow learning the lessons appropriate to it, or it is pointless for us to learn about it." Accepting this, let's take a look at the many tools at your disposal.

IN THE MOMENT

Take a moment to recall a situation in which you felt content or joyful.

•What aspects of that moment do you think most contributed to your happiness?

•What mind-set allowed you to experience those positive emotions?

•How might you access that mind-set in any circumstance, not just that particular moment?

The Tool Kit

Of all the Stoic tools you will receive, the Dichotomy of Control is the most fundamental. Its premise: Some things are in your control, and some things are outside of your control. Stoics divide every situation according to this and focus only on the former. This simple practice represents the core of a Stoic's orientation to the world. It helps you decide where to place your attention, so your actions are effective. Every practice, meditation, and action begin by training your attention on that which you can control.

Stoic training centers around three disciplines and four virtues.

•The disciplines provide the training needed to develop a Stoic outlook.

•The virtues give a definition of excellence, so you have a vision to work toward.

The three disciplines seem to have been developed by Epictetus both to inform Stoic practice and to act as a structure for his school's curriculum. We know that it was influential enough to have impacted Marcus Aurelius; he clearly references this threefold perspective throughout his writing.

The Stoics inherited the four virtues from a longer tradition that extends at least as far back as Plato and Socrates, although it's quite likely that this structure is even older.

DISCIPLINES

Here's a brief overview of the three Stoic disciplines

•The Discipline of Desire entails a radical realignment of your values as you work to desire only what is within your complete control. Redirecting your attention in this way will free you from chasing after things that do not contribute to your happiness.

•The Discipline of Action relates to your interactions with other people. The aim is to seek healthy, positive relationships with everyone you meet, even knowing others may not reciprocate.

•The Discipline of Assent concerns your thoughts about life. You learn to separate your initial reactions to the world from your final judgments about the world. You refuse to walk down mental paths that lead to negativity, instead evaluating your thoughts in order to align with wisdom.

Within each of the disciplines, you find a variety of techniques that help you cultivate a healthy mental life.

Consider this: How would it feel to have a consistently positive mental outlook?

VIRTUES

A core belief that separates Stoic thought from most other ancient philosophies—and modern ones—is that virtue is the only good. Stoics claim that only virtue is good in all circumstances. Justice is always good. Wisdom is never bad. The things many consider "good"—money, fame, and even health—can work to your benefit, no doubt, but can also play out in damaging ways. Stoicism challenges you to focus on virtue, because when you are your best self you will use the stuff of life in the best way.

Consider this: What would you say is the greatest good in life?

Rules to Live By

Remember: Your mind is yours—and yours alone. If you focus on healthy thoughts and develop balanced opinions about your situation, you will cultivate positive emotions and find lasting enthusiasm to live your best life. You will see negativity for what it is: a waste of energy. You will learn to stop allowing fear, anger, and other anxieties to grow. You will discover not only that you can weather challenges, but you often find them enjoyable. As you move in this direction, the work of being yourself will become a joy. To gain all of this, you simply need the right tools and the will to use them.

Conclusion

C an we bring the principles of Stoicism into our everyday modern life? Can some philosophers who lived so very long ago truly address our 21st century issues and problems?

Yes, we can. And they can be a huge help in dealing with our modern lifestyle.

Stoicism offers concrete solutions to human problems. Not only for the problems of ancient life nor for the problems of modern society, rather has it addressed the problems of humanity. There are constants that exist throughout the human race, and I speak not of the big ones we all know about, like love and hate and peace and war — a lot of these constants are the incredibly stressful things familiar to each of us.

You must have learned that Stoicism is a branch of philosophy created for people living in the real world. The ancient stoicism philosophers came from diverse backgrounds. For example, there was a famous stoic playwright; one was a water carrier; there was an emperor, and another one was a slave. Other stoic philosophers consisted of famous senators, soldiers, and wealthy merchants. However, they all had one thing in common; they focused on when they could control, as opposed to the external world.

Stoicism is not about suppressing emotions and feelings. Doing this often leads to disappointment and more suffering. Emotions and expectations are not the issues; rather, it is how one handles them and reacts. It is not wrong to feel and hope for a certain outcome, as long as one understands the things or circumstances that one can control and those that one cannot control.

Stoic reflection follows the philosophy of stoicism, which is centered on self-improvement. Human beings should adjust to living in the world as it is instead of trying to change it. They should find peace and clarity in the midst of all the chaos around them.

The next step is to live in accordance with the principles and philosophies of stoicism since these are of great value.

CPSIA information can be obtained
at www.ICGtesting.com
Printed in the USA
LVHW052148280621
691354LV00003B/169

9 781802 539813